this book belongs to

_____

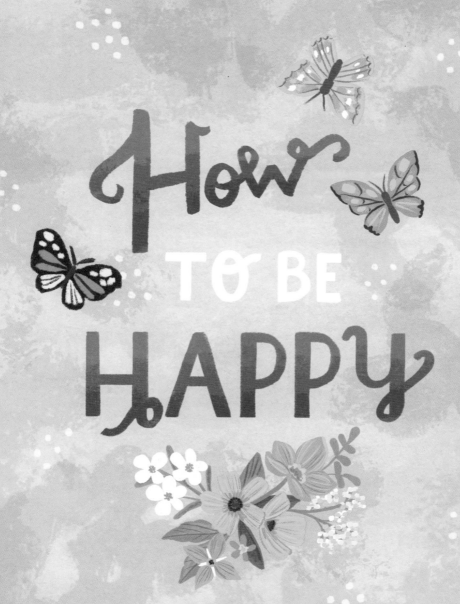

How TO BE HAPPY

OLIVIA GIBBS

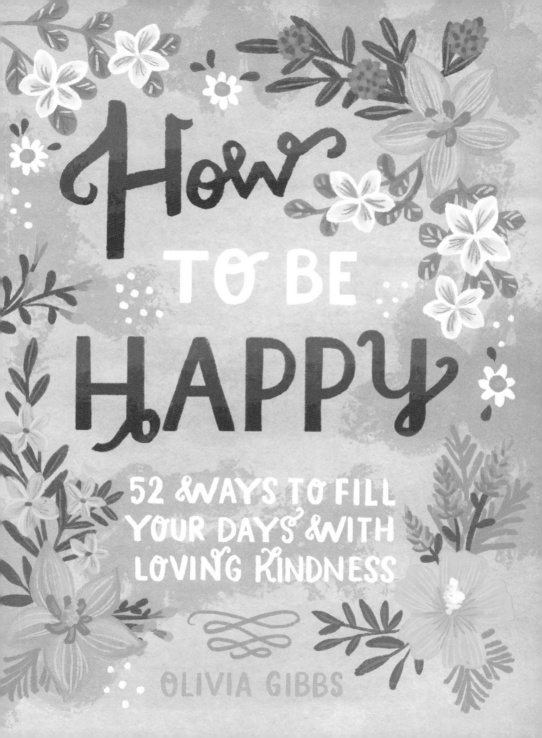

How

TO BE

HAPPY

52 WAYS TO FILL YOUR DAYS WITH LOVING KINDNESS

OLIVIA GIBBS

Illustrations by Olivia Gibbs
Book design by Michael Douglas

ISBN: 978-0-7643-6413-6
Printed in China
Copublished by Better Day Books and Schiffer Publishing, Ltd.

BETTER DAY BOOKS®

Schiffer Publishing
4880 Lower Valley Road
Atglen, PA 19310
Phone: 610-593-1777
Fax: 610-593-2002
Email: Info@schifferbooks.com
Web: www.schifferbooks.com

This title is available for promotional or
commercial use, including special editions.
Contact info@schifferbooks.com for more information.

To my husband, thank you for
your love and continued support
and encouragement.

Contents

Seek Joy

Some ways to learn to rejoice
in the well-being of others.

Keep Calm

Some ways to maintain mental calmness
and composure in difficult situations.

Spread Kindness

Some ways to spread random kindness
to others.

Kindness Cards

Spread kindness with these tear-and-share cards.
Give them to others or keep them for yourself!

Welcome

I am so grateful you have found this book. Before you dig into the coming pages, I would love to share the story about what inspired me to write it and how it has changed me for the better. I hope it will have a similar positive impact on you.

At the beginning of 2020 (during the COVID-19 pandemic), I noticed how social media and the daily news were depleting my energy. As a result, I became fearful and hopeless. So, I decided to make a conscious effort to look for hopeful and uplifting news stories worldwide. Although a lot of the reporting was bleak, I could always find joyful stories that put a smile on my face.

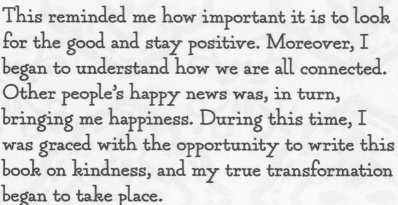

This reminded me how important it is to look for the good and stay positive. Moreover, I began to understand how we are all connected. Other people's happy news was, in turn, bringing me happiness. During this time, I was graced with the opportunity to write this book on kindness, and my true transformation began to take place.

The word "kindness" had always been one that I couldn't fully understand. It is a word that people use a lot, but everyone has a different interpretation. I was curious to dig into the concept of kindness at a deeper level. So I started my research. Soon, I discovered a more expansive concept: the Four Limitless Qualities. They are Loving Kindness, Compassion, Sympathetic Joy, and Calm. In Buddhism, they are the most important virtues because they represent love and goodwill toward everything and everybody. By practicing them, we invite positivity and love into our hearts. And, by doing so, we achieve true happiness. I immediately knew that it was the direction I wanted for the book.

As I started to practice this method, I noticed it changed how my brain worked. In everyday situations where I would have resorted to sarcasm, negativity, or even anger, I used other tools instead. Very soon, I began to notice feelings of true joy, and I was feeling completely grateful. If I saw something that made me angry, I would quickly change my perspective and calm down. I wasn't hostile, and I allowed room for other opinions and experiences.

Because we live in very uncertain times, I believe it is now that we need to rise and be a better version of ourselves. We need to be the change we want to see in the world.

I hope that reading this book will also inspire you to practice loving kindness toward yourself and others. Some of the 52 ideas included will resonate with you more than others, and that's okay. Embrace the ones you feel most drawn to, and always remember that even small changes can have a massive impact on our outlook.

I hope that this book will open your heart and bring you true happiness, just as it did for me.

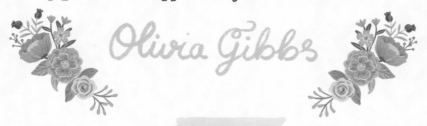

Olivia Gibbs

Meditation for LOVING KINDNESS

When we practice loving-kindness meditation, we develop a warm acceptance toward ourselves and others. It is as simple as bringing the image of a person to mind and picturing them full of happiness. You can use this meditation for yourself or anyone else.

To begin this meditation, sit in a comfortable chair (or lie down). Breathe in and out. Notice how your chest and abdomen expand and contract with each breath. When you feel relaxed, repeat the loving-kindness mantra:

May I be well and happy.

Start the meditation with yourself and then expand it by shifting your attention

1. to a loved one.
2. to someone about whom you feel neutral.
3. to someone you dislike.
4. to the rest of the world.

Be a friend

Friends are people you share your experiences with, and are an essential part of each other's lives. Good friends are loyal and trustworthy and accept you for who you are during the good and bad times.

A good friend is one who overlooks your broken fence and admires the flowers in your garden.

—Unknown

Crystals

Healing crystals are an amazing tool for enhancing and cultivating loving kindness. You can keep them with you, hold on to them, use them as jewelry, or use them to enhance your meditations. These are some of the most important ones for loving kindness.

ROSE QUARTZ

Rose quartz is known as the stone of the heart because it brings you every expression of love, including romantic love, self-love, familial love, and love for friends and humanity in general.

AMETHYST

Amethyst is a natural stress reliever that also encourages inner strength, spirituality, and intuition. It attracts positive energy while ridding the body or your home of negative energy.

AMAZONITE

Amazonite is a wonderful healer for the emotional body. It soothes trauma, calms the mind, alleviates worry and fear, and directs anger and irritability into positive action.

EMERALD

Emerald opens and nurtures the heart. It brings freshness and vitality to the spirit. A stone of inspiration and infinite patience, it embodies unity, compassion, and unconditional love.

Cultivate GRATITUDE

Gratitude is a powerful positive force and can have a substantial impact on your emotional and physical health. It helps you focus on the good things in your life and pay no attention to the things you might lack. So how can you cultivate it, and how can it help you grow kindness?

Finish each day by thinking about what made you feel grateful. You can focus on things, but I recommend directing your focus on other people. Did someone do something thoughtful for you today? Did someone help you? How did it make you feel? Gratitude helps us remember the power of each good action.

Keep a gratitude journal by your bed and spend a few minutes filling it out each night. That way, you will go to sleep happier and more at peace.

TALKING bad about OTHERS says MORE about YOU than it does about other PEOPLE

Don't TALK bad about OTHERS

Sometimes it's hard not to express negative emotions about someone who is causing us pain. So the next time you feel the urge to speak unkindly about someone, try this instead:

- Sit still and clear your mind, then take a few breaths.
- Acknowledge that this person has their own struggles.
- Repeat this loving-kindness mantra.

{

MAY

_____

(insert the person's name)

BE WELL AND HAPPY.

}

After a few minutes, notice how your body and mind change. You have turned a negative feeling into a kind one.

Express Love

By giving and expressing our love, we end up receiving more love.

Loving without reservation, listening deeply, and being present mentally and physically are all examples of loving kindness. If you love someone, be sure not only to tell them but also show them.

Giving a little kiss, thoughtful gift, or small treat is a beautiful way to show someone you care. But, of course, the best way to let someone know they matter is simply to be there for them consistently. Spend quality time with the people you love, and create new memories.

find the GOOD

Good is all around us if we look for it. The next time something negative happens, do not get triggered. Catch yourself and, instead, repeat this mantra.

EVERY day is a GOOD day.
EVERYTHING is a GOOD thing.
EVERY place is a GOOD place.
EVERY person is a GOOD person.

—Yuan Tze

..I'M LETTING GO..

...forgiveness...

Forgiveness is a conscious and deliberate decision to release feelings of resentment or vengeance toward a person, regardless of whether they deserve it. By forgiving, you bring peace, happiness, and emotional and spiritual healing into your life.

HOW CAN YOU FORGIVE?
It always helps to be still. Talk to yourself and listen. You can also keep a journal. By writing about it, you get it out of your mind and understand it. Ask yourself, Why did they do it? Was it on purpose? And if you think it was intentional, acknowledge that the person had their own struggles and problems in life.

They tried to hurt you, but it only showed their pain. Ultimately know that this person has a desire and yearning to be well and happy, just like you.

Forgiving is an inside process, but you can extend loving kindness by letting someone know that you forgive them.

Include OTHERS

It feels so awful when you are left out, not invited, or snubbed in a conversation. Because we all know how that feels, we need to be the first ones to include others that are left out.

Make sure to include others in your conversation by making eye contact or asking them something. If you are planning an event, reach out to friends you think would like to attend. Also, remember to check in with those friends you haven't seen in a while. Sometimes that is enough to show them that you care and that they matter.

Sometimes the greatest GIFT you can give ANOTHER person is to simply INCLUDE them.

Learn to Listen

Practice listening to understand vs. listening to respond. Start by putting your phone away when someone is talking to you. Make eye contact. Don't assume that you already know what the person is going to say. And don't be judgmental, and avoid jumping to conclusions.

When you listen to understand, you withhold your thoughts and feelings unless they are requested. Some people only want to be heard. So don't give your opinion unless they ask you for it.

Listening to understand is critical with kids and teenagers in your life. Because more than anyone else, they want to feel that they are important to you.

Look for the GOOD in YOURSELF

If you have a hard time seeing the good in yourself, try these ideas.

Be mindful of the good things that you do each day (in thought and deed). Also, pay attention to any compliments you receive. You can also look back to your past; what were you good at and passionate about when you were young? Finally, ask someone you trust what good they see in you.

To know yourself better, you need to spend time with yourself. That means to sit still and be quiet. It is worth knowing what makes you unique and the good that goes with that.

...everything is BEAUTIFUL when you STOP looking for FLAWS...

Write down a list of good things about you.
Keep this list as a reminder whenever you are
starting to feel down and negative about yourself.

THERE'S no TIME to be BORED in a WORLD as BEAUTIFUL as THIS

no MORE
boredom

An excellent opportunity to practice loving kindness is when you have free time. So the next time you feel boredom and dullness in your life, take a moment to appreciate it. Shift your awareness to the world around you and fill yourself with all the beauty of your surroundings.

{ the cure for
BOREDOM
is
CURIOSITY
—DOROTHY PARKER }

Plant a Garden

×××××××××××××××

Taking care of a garden and nurturing it gives you peace of mind. It makes you more connected to nature, reduces stress, and ultimately increases your happiness.

THE GLORY OF GARDENING:

hands on the dirt, head in the sun, heart with nature.
To nurture a garden is to feed not just the body, but the soul.

— Alfred Austin

My Notes

Meditation for COMPASSION

This meditation focuses on those who are suffering. It works the same way as the loving-kindness meditation, except this time, you will focus on bringing healing to the person rather than joy.

To begin this meditation, sit in a comfortable chair (or lie down). Breathe in and out. Notice how your chest and abdomen expand and contract with each breath. When you feel relaxed, repeat the compassion mantra:

> May I be free of suffering and
> the source of suffering.

Start the meditation with yourself and then expand it by shifting your attention

1. to a loved one.
2. to someone about whom you feel neutral.
3. to someone you dislike.
4. to the rest of the world.

MAY YOU BE FREE OF SUFFERING

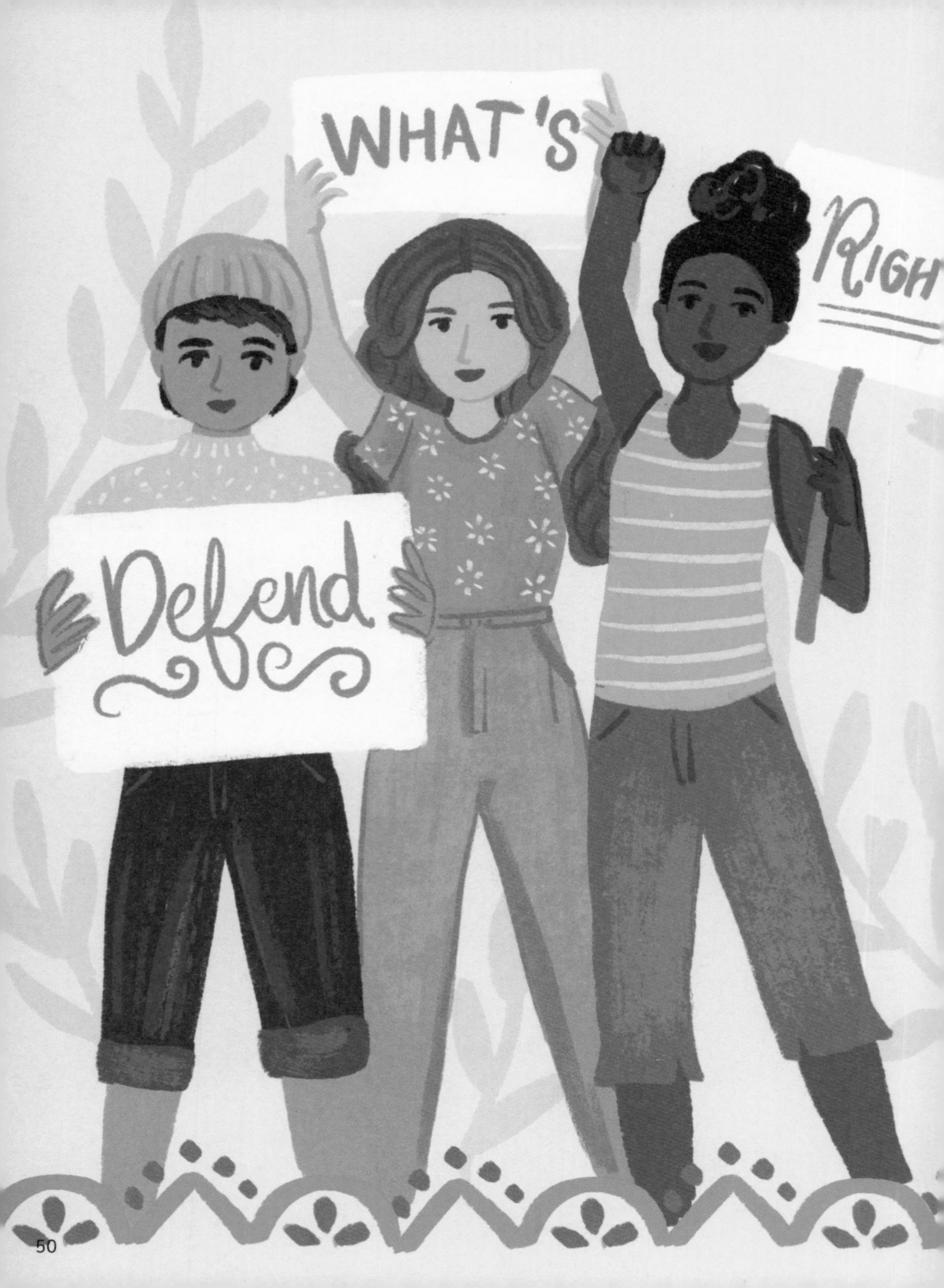
WHAT'S
RIGH
Defend

ADVOCATE

An advocate is a person who publicly supports or recommends a particular cause or policy. Every time you speak up for yourself or others, you are an advocate. Be brave and defend the rights of another person.

When the World is SILENT, even one VOICE becomes POWERFUL.
– Malala Yousafzai

BE KIND to YOURSELF

Make sure you always treat yourself the way you would treat a loved one. Instead of being critical, always be supportive and warm. So, the next time you catch yourself talking down or being tough on yourself, stop and ask yourself: "Is this the way I would talk to my loved ones?"

YOU yourself, as much as anybody in the entire universe, deserve your love and affection.

—BUDDHA

Celebrate
DIVERSITY

Celebrating diversity means understanding that each individual is unique and recognizing our differences. These differences can be age, ethnicity, gender, physical abilities, political beliefs, race, religious beliefs, sexual orientation, socio-economic status, or other ideologies.

Some Ways to Celebrate Diversity:

1. Rent a movie or read a book from another country or religion than your own.
2. Explore the music of a different culture.
3. Invite people from a different culture and share their customs.
4. Go to a restaurant serving a type of cuisine you've never had before.
5. Visit an art exhibit or a museum dedicated to other cultures.
6. Learn about traditional celebrations from other cultures.

Motivate OTHERS

When someone is working hard or trying to do something right, let them know that you noticed. Share your positive feelings as soon as they arise. Be sure to praise the effort and the progress, even if it is small.

WE RISE BY
Lifting
OTHERS
-ROBERT INGERSOLL

Being SCARED is PART of Being ALIVE

ACCEPT IT

and Walk THROUGH IT

— Robin Sharma

Let GO of Fears

A significant source of suffering is our fears. And in reality, our fears are just like any other thoughts. We have them, we are not them, and we should try to let them go.

Get the courage to write them down. Go into details, and try to find blockages in different parts of your life. You may uncover fears you did not realize you had.

Make a list of your worries and then analyze each one of them. Why are you afraid? What would happen if you faced your fears? How would that make you feel?

Mindful EATING

×××××   ×××××××

Mindful eating means being fully aware of the food and drink you put into your body while doing it. It involves noticing how the food makes you feel, and your body's signals about taste, satisfaction, and fullness. It can also extend to the process of buying, preparing, and serving your food, as well as eating it.

HOW TO PRACTICE MINDFUL EATING

- Eat more slowly and don't rush your meals.
- Chew thoroughly.
- Eliminate distractions by turning off the TV and putting down your phone.
- Eat in silence.
- Focus on how the food makes you feel.
- Stop eating when you're full.
- Enjoy preparing your food as well as consuming it.

Emotions are the LANGUAGE of the SOUL

—KARLA MCLAREN

NURTURE your EMOTIONS

Being emotionally healthy doesn't mean you're happy all the time. It means you're aware of your emotions, whether they are positive or negative. And the more you are aware, the more you understand yourself and understand others.

How can you nurture your emotions? Spend quality time with yourself. Tune into how you feel during different situations throughout the day. Talk to yourself or write in a journal. Spend time doing something you love, like practicing a hobby, and see how that makes you feel. Or see how doing your everyday routine tasks makes you feel. What situations trigger anger, sadness, or frustration, and why? Try to explain your thoughts and emotions. By doing that, it becomes easier to understand them and manage them.

NURTURE your INNER CHILD

We all have an inner child. You might think of this inner child as a representation of yourself when you were young, or as a collection of the different stages you've lived through, or a symbol of your carefree dreams and playfulness.

Sometimes your inner child was hurt and now needs protection. You can work on healing your inner child by starting a dialogue with your younger self. First, ask some questions such as: How do you feel? How can I support you? What do you need from me? Then, write your answers in a journal. It may seem awkward at first, but knowing your inner child is a part of knowing yourself.

Put YOURSELF in other PEOPLE'S SHOES

We sometimes add to our pain and suffering because we are overly sensitive and take things too personally. The next time you encounter a difficult situation with someone, make an effort to imagine how you would feel or act if you were in their position. You never know what is going on in another person's life. By opening your mind to this kind of empathetic thinking, you open yourself up to kindness and understanding.

When you learn to walk in other people's shoes, you open your heart to kindness.

VOLUNTEER

When you volunteer, you are doing good for others and the community. In addition, it keeps you connected and provides a natural sense of accomplishment, which is ultimately great for your mind and body.

You can start by researching volunteer opportunities in your community.

Check your county website for volunteer opportunities. Other common places that usually have volunteer opportunities are homeless shelters, animal shelters, retirement homes, and libraries.

My Notes

Meditation for
SEEKING JOY

This meditation focuses on rejoicing in the well-being of others. Think of someone you know that always seems joyful and in a happy mood. We will bring this person to mind and focus on the good cheer and lightness this person brings to others and the environment. And as we do this, we will enter into the same joy, share it, and rejoice in it.

To begin this meditation, sit in a comfortable chair (or lie down). Breathe in and out. Notice how your chest and abdomen expand and contract with each breath. When you feel relaxed, repeat this mantra:

We are all one. Your joy is my joy.
Your success is my success.

CELEBRATE other PEOPLE'S SUCCESS

When we celebrate others' successes as if they were our own, we feel a massive surge in positivity and joy.

HELP OTHERS Celebrate their Happiness. HAPPINESS is not limited; HAPPINESS GROWS Happiness.

COMPARISON IS the THIEF of JOY

DON'T COMPARE
Yourself

One of the enemies of seeking joy is comparing yourself to others. You are never going to be better than others in every way. Life is about getting inspired by others. Instead of trying to be as good as or better than them, focus your energy on being the very best version of yourself. Use their successes to be motivated.

Next time you catch yourself using someone else as a benchmark for your worth, stop and redirect your energy and attention to your own goals and what is required to achieve them. Then, you can repeat this mantra to yourself:

Nobody is me; I walk my own path

We don't STOP PLAYING because WE GROW OLD WE GROW OLD because WE STOP PLAYING

—GEORGE BERNARD SHAW

PLAY & LAUGH
together

You are never too old to play. Playing together is a magical way to build connections. When you play and have fun with someone, you are bonding with them. So whether you are with your family, friends, or children, don't be afraid to get silly and fill your life with more joy. Laughter can change a bad mood!

SEE
the BIGGER PICTURE

The opposite of feeling joy for another is jealousy. If you feel envious of someone, remember that they have experienced challenges and struggles just like you. When you expand your perspective to think about another person's more extensive life journey, you can feel true joy for them.

HE WHO ENVIES OTHERS, DOES NOT OBTAIN PEACE.
—BUDDHA

WATCH A CHILD
or
ANIMAL PLAY

There is a lot that adults can learn from watching children or animals play. Both approach situations with curiosity and energy. And they are easy to express joy and excitement. Just by watching them, you can tune into that same joy!

Seeing the world through the eyes of a child is the purest joy that anyone can experience.
— Constance Zimmer

My notes

Meditation for KEEPING CALM

This meditation focuses on maintaining mental calmness, composure, and evenness of temper, especially in a difficult situation. You can focus this meditation on yourself. But it can also be extended to others.

To begin this meditation, sit in a comfortable chair (or lie down). Breathe in and out. Notice how your chest and abdomen expand and contract with each breath. When you feel relaxed, repeat this mantra:

May I accept things just as they are.
May I accept myself just as I am.

MAY I ACCEPT THINGS AS THEY ARE

Aromatherapy

Subtle aromatherapy allows you to use essential oils with sensitivity and intention in your personal and spiritual growth. Here are some essential oils that you can use alone or mixed.

ROSE

Rose brings in positive energy and promotes love, compassion, hope, and patience. It also encourages creativity and a love of beauty.

LAVENDER

Lavender balances the energy centers and calms. It clears energy blocks and brings in positivity.

BERGAMOT

Bergamot attracts positive energy and eases grief. It also promotes self-love.

CARDAMON

Cardamon promotes enthusiasm.

FRANKINCENSE

Frankincense quiets and clarifies the mind.

BE PATIENT

Having patience means being able to wait calmly in the face of frustration or adversity. Being patient is a skill, and to perfect it; you need to practice.

There are many opportunities to practice patience every day.

So, the next time you catch yourself getting agitated while driving or waiting in line, stop and repeat this mantra to yourself.

{ I am filled with PATIENCE and PEACE }

When we
RETURN
to our
BREATHING,
we return to the
PRESENT moment,
our TRUE
Home.
—THICH NHAT HANH

BE PRESENT

Being in the present moment, or the "here and now," means that we are aware and mindful of what is happening at this very moment. We are not distracted by the past or worried about the future.

1. Start by paying attention to your breathing; do not try to change it. Just observe it.

2. You can continue with a body scan. Start from your feet and work your way up to the head. Are there some parts of your body that feel tenser? Are you relaxed?

3. You can end by becoming aware of your surroundings. Warm? Hard? Are you lying down? How does the part of the body that is touching the surface feel? Are there any noises nearby? Don't judge them; be aware of them.

Another opportunity to practice being in the present is when performing everyday chores. For example, when you wash the dishes, do not think of how much work it is. Instead, focus on how the warm water and soap feel on your hand. By removing the purpose of the chore, you can remain in the present moment and even enjoy it.

A walk in nature
walks the soul back home.
—MARY DAVIS

Connect to Nature

Nature is inherently peaceful, calm, and beautiful. Everything is perfectly in balance. So, how can we feel more in tune with nature?

Grounding

or earthing: These are creative ways to reconnect to Earth and its balance electrically. Let the bottoms of your feet, palms of your hands, or entire body touch the Earth. Walk barefoot in the grass, lie down on the sand, or swim in the ocean.

Forest Bathing

Head out to a park, nature trail, lake, or forest to fully surround yourself with nature. When you get there, take a few deep breaths and feel the clean oxygen filling your chest. Now take in all of the beauty around you. Take time to observe. Just be fully in the moment while bathing all your senses in nature.

EMBRACE CHANGE

Change is an opportunity for you to experience something new and to grow and evolve as a person.

One way to not be afraid of the change that awaits you is to be aware of the change that has already happened in your life. Start by writing down the changes you have faced. How did you feel about them? How did they end up? Can you learn something from them?

the SECRET of CHANGE is to focus all of your ENERGY not on fighting the OLD but on building the NEW.

—SOCRATES

ENJOY SILENCE

Allow yourself to spend some time throughout the day in absolute silence. Don't use your phone or television, and do not think about what to do next. Silence allows you to relax and restore.

"Silence is something that comes from your heart, not from outside. Silence doesn't mean not talking and not doing things; it means that you are not disturbed inside. If you are truly silent, then no matter what situation you find yourself in, you can enjoy the silence. We spend a lot of time looking for happiness when the world right around us is full of wonder. There is beauty calling to us every day, every hour, but we are rarely in a position to listen. The basic condition for us to be able to hear the call of beauty and respond to it is silence. If we don't have silence in ourselves — if our mind, our body, is full of noise — then we can't hear beauty's call."

—Thich Nhat Hanh, *Silence*

an

OPEN

Heart

... is an ...

OPEN

mind

—DALAI LAMA XIV

KEEP an OPEN MIND

Open-mindedness involves being open to new experiences, ideas, people, theories, and ways of living. Being open can help inspire a more optimistic attitude toward life and the future.

You can train your brain to be more open-minded by getting out of your comfort zone more often. Here are three easy ways:

1. Listen to a new kind of music.
2. Dine at a new restaurant or order a different menu item.
3. Watch a new kind of movie.

You can also train your brain by reframing negative thoughts. For example, instead of jumping to a fast "no" when asked to try something new, ask yourself, "Why not?" What would happen if I tried?"

RELAX

There are many different ways to relax, so it is good to practice various techniques to see what works best for you. These are some ideas.

BREATHING EXERCISES

Breathe in to a slow count of three, and then breathe out to the same slow count of three. Feel your belly rise and fall as you breathe in and out. Repeat this exercise five times or as long as you need to feel relaxed.

USE YOUR IMAGINATION

Close your eyes and imagine yourself in a serene setting. Now imagine all the details linked to that place: the sights, sounds, smells, tastes, and tactile feelings. The more you get into the visualization, the more you will relax.

WRITE IT DOWN

Keep a journal handy and write down whatever is making you stressed, nervous, or agitated.

RELEASE TENSION

Tense up parts of your body for a few seconds and then release them. Notice how your body sensations change.

✕ ✕ ✕ ✕ ✕ ✕ ✕ ✕ ✕ ✕ ✕ ✕ ✕ ✕ ✕ ✕ ✕

My Notes

Spread

kindness

MY HAPPINESS GROWS WHEN I SHARE IT WITH YOU

SHARE YOUR
Happiness

Sometimes we block our happiness and successes because we don't want to make others feel worse about themselves. But like Gautama Buddha said: "Thousands of candles can be lit from a single candle. Happiness never decreases by being shared."

So, the next time you feel yourself trying to block your happiness, try repeating this loving-kindness phrase instead.

My happiness grows when I share it with you

a WARM SMILE is the UNIVERSAL language KINDNESS

—WILLIAM ARTHUR WARD

SMILE

Smile at people. Smiling can inspire others to smile.
And smiling has positive effects on you as well!
It is one of the easiest ways to show kindness.

The Dalai Lama said: "My practice when I see
someone is to smile."

As a little experiment, smile right this moment
and see what happens. Many studies show how you
can trick the brain into thinking you are happier
just putting on a smile. And if that's not reason
enough, smiling can also reduce your stress and
boost your immune system!

*My practice when I
see someone, is to smile
—Dalai Lama XIV*

no NEGATIVITY

Feelings are contagious, both good feelings and bad feelings. So be careful when you are around negativity. When possible, walk away from negative thoughts and negative people.

The next time someone tries to throw their anger at you, do not let it pass through you. Instead, take a couple of breaths and respond with this mantra.

You give me your anger but I do not accept it. Instead, I wish you happiness.

COMPLIMENT
PEOPLE wherever you go.
PRAISE every single thing
you see.
BE a ray of SUNSHINE
to everyone you
MEET.
—RHONDA BYRNE

130

Compliment SOMEONE

Compliments help us express the appreciation we feel to others. When we receive compliments, they make us feel valued. When we get in the habit of giving compliments, it helps us appreciate the world around us. In turn, we get used to seeing the good in others.

Never underestimate the power of a random compliment.

BE KIND to the Environment

We all have an impact on the environment. And there are many ways that we can help. Here are some examples:

- Reduce, reuse, and recycle.
- Cut down on the amount of trash you throw away.
- Use reusable shopping bags.
- Pick up trash and put it in the trash can.
- Use reusable beverage containers.
- Avoid using plastic straws.
- Switch to electronic bills to reduce paper.
- Turn off lights or electronics when they are not in use.
- Do not waste water.
- Carpool, use public transportation or ride a bike.

The Earth is what we all have in common.
—WENDELL BERRY

OFFER HELP

No one is USELESS in this WORLD WHO LIGHTENS the BURDENS of ANOTHER.

–CHARLES DICKENS

SHOP SMALL

Behind every small business, there is a hard working family in your community. There are different ways you can help them out.

BUY SMALL:
Visit local shops and make purchases.

WRITE REVIEWS:
Leave a kind review after your visit. Even if you do not make a purchase, you can leave a positive review about your experience.

SPREAD THE WORD:
Many small businesses struggle with marketing, so if you like the store, make sure to tell others.

Be Kind to your NEIGHBOR

Be friendly: When you see your neighbor, show them your smile. Say hello or wave to greet them.

Offer help: If you know the neighbors are going on vacation, you can offer to pick up the mail, take out the trash, water the plants, or just keep an eye on the house.

Help with the yard: Yard work is physically demanding, so lend a hand if you have a neighbor who needs help. Consider mowing their lawn, helping to pull weeds, or watering plants.

Leave a note: You can leave a friendly note on their mailbox, or if you have children, encourage them to chalk a fun message on their driveway.

Respect boundaries: Always make sure you know what boundaries your neighbors have and respect them.

SEND thank you NOTES

There is no better way to show your gratitude than saying thank you. Never forget to thank all the special people that are part of our lives.

TEACHERS

Health Workers

RETAIL WORKERS

FRIENDS

Significant Others

PARENTS

Children

HELPING HANDS

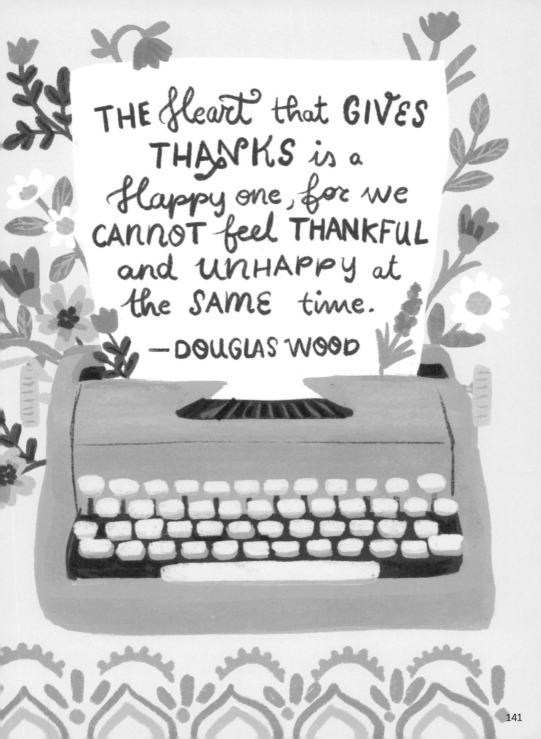

THE Heart that GIVES THANKS is a Happy one, for we CANNOT feel THANKFUL and UNHAPPY at the SAME time.

—DOUGLAS WOOD

WRITE Encouragement NOTES

Leave random notes in surprising places to brighten someone's day! You can make your cards or use the ones at the back of this book. Here are some places you can leave them:

- in a doctor's office
- in a library book
- inside magazines
- on a neighbor's mailbox
- on a shopping cart
- on a store shelf
- on a stranger's car
- Or, pick a random address and mail it!

You
MAKE
the WORLD
a better
PLACE

BUY a friend FLOWERS

Did you know that flowers have meanings? They make lovely gifts, and they are wonderful for any occasion. Here are some flowers that mean loving kindness:

ALSTROEMERIA
Alstroemerias represent a strong bond and prosperity.

LILY OF THE VALLEY
This flower represents happiness.

ORCHID
Orchids bring good luck and prosperity.

PINK ROSE
These buds symbolize happiness, gratitude, and admiration.

SUNFLOWER
Sunflowers represent adoration and loyalty.

TULIP
Tulips represent perfect and deep love.

VIOLET
Violets represent modesty and faithfulness.

ZINNIA
Zinnias represent everlasting friendship.

OTHER SMALL ACTS
of Kindness

- Bring a treat to work.
- Donate food to a food drive.
- Donate your old clothes.
- Help clean up a mess.
- Help someone struggling to carry their grocery bags.
- Hold the door open for a stranger.
- Hold the elevator for someone.
- Leave a snack for the mailman.
- Leave parking spots close to the store available for others.
- Leave some change in a vending machine.
- Leave unused coupons on grocery items.

- Leave your serviceperson a generous tip.
- Lend a friend your favorite movie or book.
- Let someone cut in front of you in line.
- Offer to return a stranger's grocery cart to the front of the store.
- Pay for someone else's coffee or meal.
- Put coins in an expired parking meter.
- Say yes when the cashier asks you to donate to a cause.
- Slow down so someone can merge in front of you in traffic.
- Snap a photo for a family.

KEEP a KINDNESS TRACKER

Keep a Kindness Tracker for a week to make sure you get in the habit of practicing loving kindness. Then, fill in the seven tracker forms on the following pages. And try to at least complete three different acts per day.

EXAMPLE DAY

- Practiced Loving kindness meditation.
- I used recycled shopping bags at the supermarket.
- I left a snack and thank-you card to the mailman.

DAY 1

DAY 2

DAY 3

DAY 4

DAY 5

DAY 6

YAY!! YOU DID IT

My notes

Happiness TRACKER

Now that you have finished the book, it's time to try the ideas! Use the Happiness Tracker on the following pages to monitor your progress. Mark a check next to each entry as you feel you have successfully adopted it into your life.

Loving Kindness

- [ ] Loving-Kindness Meditation
- [ ] Look for the Good in Yourself
- [ ] Cultivate Gratitude
- [ ] Learn to Listen
- [ ] No More Boredom
- [ ] Include Others

- [ ] Don't Talk Bad about Others
- [ ] Forgiveness
- [ ] Find the Good
- [ ] Express Love
- [ ] Be a Friend
- [ ] Plant a Garden
- [ ] Use Crystals

Compassion

- [ ] Compassion Meditation
- [ ] Be Kind to Yourself
- [ ] Let Go of Fears
- [ ] Mindful Eating
- [ ] Nurture Your Emotions
- [ ] Nurture Your Inner Child

- [ ] Motivate Others
- [ ] Advocate
- [ ] Volunteer
- [ ] Celebrate Diversity
- [ ] Put Yourself in Other People's Shoes

Seek Joy

- ☐ Seeking-Joy Meditation
- ☐ Play and Laugh Together
- ☐ Don't Compare Yourself
- ☐ Celebrate Other People's Success
- ☐ Watch a Child or Animal Play
- ☐ See the Bigger Picture

Keep Calm

- ☐ Keeping-Calm Meditation
- ☐ Relax
- ☐ Be Patient
- ☐ Connect to Nature
- ☐ Keep an Open Mind
- ☐ Embrace Change
- ☐ Enjoy Silence
- ☐ Be Present
- ☐ Aromatherapy

Spread Kindness

- ☐ Share Your Happiness
- ☐ Smile
- ☐ No Negativity
- ☐ Compliment Someone
- ☐ Be Kind to the Environment
- ☐ Offer Help
- ☐ Be Kind to Your Neighbor
- ☐ Buy a Friend Flowers
- ☐ Shop Small
- ☐ Send Thank-You Notes
- ☐ Write Encouragement Notes
- ☐ Other Small Acts of Kindness

ABOUT THE AUTHOR

Olivia Gibbs is an illustrator and surface pattern
designer from Spain living in Kansas.

Her work can be found on many different products, from
greeting cards and wall art to home decor and fabric.

She lives with her husband and two daughters.

When not working on her art, she loves to travel,
read, and spend time with her loved ones.

www.oliviagibbs.com

MORE INSPIRATION!

If you love this book, please also check out
The Better Day Book by Olivia Gibbs.
It features 52 illustrated ideas for mindfulness,
relaxation, and self-care. And, it also includes
journal pages and pull-out postcards!

Bibliography

BOOKS

B. Alan Wallace. *The Four Immeasurables:* Practices to Open the Heart. Ithaca, NY: Snow Lion, September 16, 2010.

Debbie Tenzer. *Do One Nice Thing: Little Things You Can Do to Make the World a Lot Nicer.* New York: Crown, May 5, 2009.

His Holiness the Dalai Lama and Howard C. Cutler, MD. *The Art of Happiness: A Handbook for Living.* New York: Riverhead Books, July 21, 2020.

Mary Brantley & Tesla Hanauer. *The Gift of Loving-Kindness: 100 Meditations on Compassion, Generosity, and Forgiveness.* Oakland, CA: New Harbinger, September 1, 2008.

Qing Dr. Li. *Forest Bathing: How Trees Can Help You Find Health and Happiness.* Illustrated ed. London: Penguin Life, April 17, 2018.

Thich Nhat Hanh. *Silence: The Power of Quiet in a World Full of Noise.* New York: HarperOne, January 26, 2016.

Thich Nhat Hanh. *The Miracle of Mindfulness: An Introduction to the Practice of Meditation.* Boston: Beacon, May 1, 1999.

WEBSITES

———. "15 Flowers That Mean Love to Add to Your Bouquet."
https://www.proflowers.com/blog/which-flowers-mean-love. February 10, 2020.

———. "The Family That Plays Together."
https://www.ahaparenting.com/parenting-tools/family-life/play-together.

Adda Bjarnadottir, MS, RDN (Ice). "Mindful Eating 101—a Beginner's Guide."
https://www.healthline.com/nutrition/mindful-eating-guide. June 19, 2019.

Carly Graf. "The Easiest Way to Boost Your Health? Step Outside."
http://www.parsleyhealth.com/blog/earthing-grounding-forest-bathing-benefits. November 13, 2019.

Crystal Raypole. "8 Ways to Start Healing Your Inner Child."
https://www.healthline.com/health/mental-health/inner-child-healing. July 8, 2020.

D'Arcy Lyness, PhD. "Being Your Best Self."
https://www.rchsd.org/health-articles/understanding-your-emotions/. December 2012.

Daniela Tempesta. "Why You Should Stop Comparing Yourself to Others."
https://www.huffpost.com/entry/comparing-yourself_b_4441288. February 16, 2014.

Joni Keim. "Using Subtle Aromatherapy to Promote Kindness."
https://essentialthree.com/subtle-aromatherapy-to-promote-kindness/.

Margaret Manning. "Want to Feel More Positive? Learn to Give Genuine Compliments."
https://www.happify.com/hd/learn-to-give-genuine-compliments/.

Mystic Journey Crystals. "Crystals Guide."
https://www.mysticjourneycrystals.com/crystal-guide.

Nicole Spector. "Smiling Can Trick Your Brain into Happiness—and Boost Your Health."
https://www.nbcnews.com/better/health/smiling-can-trick-your-brain-happiness-boost-your-health-ncna822591. November 28, 2017, updated January 9, 2018.

Pema Dragpa. "The Four Immeasurables."
https://www.padmasambhava.org/sermon/four-immesurables/. September 16, 2016.

Rabbhi Yahiya. "Nine ways to celebrate diversity."
https://www.britishcouncil.org/voices-magazine/nine-ways-celebrate-diversity. May 21, 2015.

Sandra Nolan. "Accept Your Journey: Stop Comparing Yourself with Others."
https://thriveglobal.com/stories/accept-your-journey-stop-comparing-yourself-with-others/. February 2, 2018.

TEAR & SHARE
Kindness
CARDS

In the coming pages, you will find 16 cards to tear and share.

Whether you are looking for a little reminder for yourself or you want to share them with others, you can use these cards to practice and spread kindness.

SOME IDEAS ON HOW YOU CAN USE THEM:

- Keep them in your wallet for daily reminders.
- Punch a hole in a corner and use them as gift tags.
- Use them to write uplifting messages and reminders.
- Leave some behind for someone random to find.

TEAR & SHARE
Kindness
CARDS

MAY I
÷ BE ÷
Well
&
Happy

MAY I
ACCEPT
things
→ AS ←
THEY ARE

YOUR
JOY
is my
JOY

MAY I
÷ BE ÷
free
OF
SUFFERING

You MAKE the WORLD a better PLACE

I AM SO thankful FOR YOU

BE
the CHANGE
YOU WISH TO SEE
in the
WORLD
-GANDHI

When We
RETURN
to our
BREATHING,
we return to the
PRESENT MOMENT,
our TRUE
Home.
-THICH NHAT HANH

I am FILLED with Patience

SO grateful WE ARE FRIENDS

BE kind to YOURSELF

BETTER DAY BOOKS®

HAPPY • CREATIVE • CURATED®

Business is personal at Better Day Books. We were founded on the belief that all people are creative and that making things by hand is inherently good for us. It's important to us that you know how much we appreciate your support. The book you are holding in your hands was crafted with the artistic passion of the author and brought to life by a team of wildly enthusiastic creatives who believed it could inspire you. If it did, please drop us a line and let us know about it. Connect with us on Instagram, post a photo of your art, and let us know what other creative pursuits you are interested in learning about. It all matters to us. You're kind of a big deal.

it's a good day to have a better day!®

www.betterdaybooks.com
better_day_books